duino elegies
rainer maria rilke

property of
marie von thurn und taxis-hohenlohe

interpretive translation
sheryl massaro

&

Duineser Elegien
Rainer Maria Rilke

Aus dem Besitz der Fürstin
Marie von Thurn und Taxis-Hohenlohe

ISBN: 979-8-9887537-0-4 (Paperback)

Library of Congress Control Number: 2023917740

Pablo Picasso, *Family of Saltimbanques*; Fifth Elegy
© 2023 Estate of Pablo Picasso/Artists Rights Society (ARS), New York

Front cover image by Sheryl Massaro
Book design by Sheryl Massaro
Font used throughout is Helvetica

Printed by DiggyPOD, Inc., in the United States of America

First printing edition 2023

Sheryl Massaro
FAC Artist Studios
7 North Market St., Suite 25
Frederick MD 21701
www.sherylmassaro.com

dedicated with gratitude to

Myra Sklarew

contents

preface

artwork

german text: pen & ink drawing, *duino castle,* title page
  by sylvia c. massaro

english text: prints of oil paintings
  by sheryl massaro:

cover   *the blue angel*
the first   *the winter angel*
the second   *yellow clouds*
the third   *on the cusp*
the fourth   *woods*
the fifth   *angels & refugees*
the sixth   *mullein field*
the seventh   *hyacinth field*
the eighth   *red slide*
the ninth   *rosy windows*
the tenth   *in the water*

preface

It is now 2023—the 100th publication anniversary of Rainer Maria Rilke's complete *Duineser Elegein* by Insel-Verlag in 1923. It's been half a century since I first met Rilke, through the 1940 translation of the *Duino Elegies* by C.F. MacIntyre. I was a very young adult, and it was in a narrow, long-gone bookstore that I walked across train tracks and through a lumberyard to reach. I read a selection from the translation every Saturday.

What kept me coming back was the feeling that this distant European had lived so purposefully with the tremendous solitude I felt and considered almost a handicap. Depression, loneliness, fear of the future were abated just from realizing that someone else, long ago, had mined similar feelings to share some inspiration and creativity with the world. For the most part, though, I had absolutely no idea what the fellow was writing about. Even after painstakingly translating the *Elegies* myself in the late 1980s, as a kind of apprenticeship after completing an MFA in Creative Writing, I still had no idea what Rilke was trying to communicate. Well, perhaps I had an *idea*, but not an *understanding*.

Rainer Karl Wilhelm Johann Josef Maria Rilke was born in Prague in 1875 and died of leukemia in a Swiss sanatorium in 1926. He was unusually sensitive, had a mother who dressed him as a girl for the first few years of his life, and a father who sent him to military school during his adolescence. As an adult, he was popular and polite. He married the sculptress Clara Westhoff and fathered daughter Ruth. He spent much of his life on his own, however, sometimes looked after by one of several female friends or a wealthy patron.

One of these patrons was Princess Marie von Thurn und Taxis-Hohenlohe who, for the winter of 1911-1912, offered Rilke the use of her Castle Duino in Trieste, Italy, overlooking the Adriatic. It was during a storm there that Rilke first heard the "voice" that guided him into the *Duino Elegies*, and that sporadically prompted him until their completion in 1922. Rilke refers to this voice as of an angel. Over the next 10 years (which included World War I), bits and pieces of the *Elegies* were composed during Rilke's travels through Spain, France, and Germany. He completed them in 1922 at Château de Muzot in Switzerland's Rhone Valley.

Rilke mastered many things during his life, and perhaps the most significant was the ability to survive on his own terms, with compassion. What attracted me those years ago to Rilke's work is that, no matter how scattered and sweeping the thoughts and images of the *Duino Elegies*, they are rooted in questions and musings that many of us relate to.

There exists in the *Elegies* a breadth of perception and experience that calls to mind the journeys of near-death survivors—a sudden comprehensive knowledge of events, thoughts—and time is nonexistent. In the *Elegies*, we are asked to forego a reliance on logic, or perhaps to experience a logic that does not have the usual constraints we are familiar with, and to be open to the concept of life as a continuum, into what we define as both our pasts and futures.

In 2022, I felt ready to tackle again the *Duino Elegies*. Why? Because the world recently had experienced a terrible pandemic, my United States was in the throes of reasserting its decency after a political debacle, the world's weather patterns had become crazed, and I saw around me young people who had become even more challenged than I had been 50 years ago. I decided to try again to make the *Elegies* more understandable to readers who needed to experience the relief and hope I had in that little bookshop in another lifetime.

What I offer here is an interpretation, rather than a new classic translation. Some of Rilke's allusions and much of his voice take a backseat to flow and clarity. I'm sure I have broken many translation "rules," but this interpretation makes the *Elegies* far more understandable to me and gives me even more respect for Rilke. It took the better part of a year to complete, and more meditation than I thought possible. I hope it resonates with other readers.

A note on my use of lower case throughout the text: this is nothing more than my contribution to equality. In my poetry, all letters are equal.

There have been several complete translations of the *Duino Elegies* into English, and I wish to acknowledge and thank the following translators whose renderings helped to guide me through my own: Elaine E. Boney (The University of North Carolina Press, 1975), J.B. Leishman and Stephen Spender (W.W. Norton & Co., Inc.,1939 and 1967), Stephen Mitchell (Random House, 1982 and Vintage, 2009), David Young (W.W. Norton & Co., Inc.,1978), C.F. MacIntyre (The University of California Press, 1940 and 2001), Edward Snow (North Point Press, 2001), Alison Croggon (Newport Street Books, 2022), Stephen Cohn (Carcanet Press, 1989), Alfred Corn (W.W. Norton & Co., Inc., 2021).

Very special thanks to the Frederick Arts Council in Frederick, Maryland, through whom I received a Create and Activate Now (C.A.N.) award from the National Endowment for the Arts, providing support for this work.

S.A.M.
May 9, 2023
Urbana, Maryland

duino elegies
rainer maria rilke

property of
marie von thurn und taxis-hohenlohe

interpretive translation
sheryl massaro

perhaps an angel rarely knows if it moves
among the living or dead. its home is eternity.

from *the first*

the first

here in mad anguish i howl,
yet if one among the clouds of angels
rushed to comfort me, i would vanish
in the embrace of those magnificent wings,
in the radiance of a pure grace
we cannot look away from,
even knowing we will be lost
in its searing light.
every angel dazzles, overwhelms.

and so i stay quiet,
still, holding my torment close,
not knowing where to turn for solace.
not to angel or man, and the animals,
who are at ease everywhere,
pity how quickly we lose
our footing in this world.
perhaps a tree we see each day
will serve to strengthen us,
one whose roots have bonded
with its slope, calmly enduring
like the pavement we walked yesterday,
as true as a habit that found us, and stayed.
or we might turn to night,
whose indigo blankness grows full
from our upturned faces as they seek
the tenderest company for loneliness.
does such elusive sweetness ever share itself?
it is already in those enamored with love.
perhaps the rest of us could shed
and fling out our emptiness
to fill the air with new spaces, new skies
where birds might swarm in delight.

every springtime has yearned
for you to love its blooming. many stars
have shone and gifted their light for you.
a tide of old memory rose beside you,
or a violin's notes sought your love. all these
were for you alone, but did you welcome them?
or were you looking elsewhere, desperate to find
that one lover every infatuation assured you was near?

(and *where* would you love her, now that your rooms
crowd with fantasies that spend the night?)
but if you do find this lover, sing to them,
praise them whose warmth stays close.
yet, you almost envy those
who no longer burn with desire.
they might be more attentive lovers
than those anxious to assay again
toward an impossibly lasting elation,
whose passions tax nature
to exhaustion and fulfillment denied.

the one we revere is the one who falters.
think of gaspara stampa, the jilted poet
whose words and rhythms reformed
her brokenness into beautiful strength.
could you or i rise above such despair?
surely such pivotal sorrows serve to guide us?
shouldn't we disentangle from lovers and,
freed, become our own intent? the way an arrow
flies from its string, becoming *more* in its arc,
never landing twice on the same mark.

voices, *voices*. listen, my heart, with the faith
of saints, who waited for the voice of God
to lift them bodily, kneeling, in complete peace.
their existence *was* their listening.
i doubt that you or i could bear the voice of God,
but there is a constant current that comes with stillness.
it is the uneasy rustlings of the newly dead, their fates
touching you in the churches of rome and naples,
or borne in deep inscriptions, as in helleman's plaque
at santa maria formosa—a man who lived for others
in life, and for himself in marble now in death.
and what does this persistent unease want from me?
to move aside the injustices that hinder our dead
from their exquisite metamorphosis.

it must be baffling to be removed from this earth,
to depart from ways of life just barely learned,
to leave behind the human meaning of future;
to become a different being,
beyond the touch of others,
even without the tether of a name,

like a plaything outgrown.
strange to *feel* nothing, to *want* nothing.
strange to see your solid form now strewn
back to the earth and stars.
and being *dead* must be tedious,
full of atoning before one can glimpse eternity.

but it might be we the living
who create such boundaries.
perhaps an angel rarely knows if it moves
among the living or dead. its home is eternity,
whose current surges through all existences,
including what we know as death.

those new to death are weaned from mortality
the way a babe outgrows a mother's breasts.
but we, whose enlightenment so often springs
from grief—could *we* live without *them*?
is the myth of linus in vain, that music was born
from the inconsolable mourning of a barren land
whose beloved near-god suddenly was taken?
there came into that desert the first surge,
the opening crescendo that still bears us on,
still soothes us, still delivers us.

            . . . and who
    could hold onto those who are beautiful?
   poses scud across their faces like clouds in sky.

                            from *the second*

the second

every angel is fearsome,
yet still i dare to summon you, knowing
you hover near us almost like birds of prey.
when the angel raphael came to tobias,
he seemed like a youth, all power
and radiance hidden for their journey.
but if such an archangel approached us now,
unshielded from behind the stars,
our astonished hearts would leap
from our breasts and be no more.
who are you?

early beauties, coddled favorites of the universe,
mountain crests, peaks reddening in the new sky
of creation—pollen of a blooming godhead,
kaleidoscopes of light, colonnades, stairs, thrones,
spaces of pulsing matter, shells of joy, clamor
of enchanted senses and suddenly, one by one,
mirrors: drawing their own gushing beauty
into their features again.

but when *we* feel, we are dispelled.
we breathe our lives in, then out and away;
ember by ember, we sputter and fade.
one might say: *oh yes*, our hearts are one,
this room, all spring is alive with you. ...
but when we caress, those we hold
lose themselves in our arms,
as we are lost in theirs. and who
could hold onto those who are beautiful?
poses scud across their faces like clouds in sky.
what we have goes away, the way dew or steam disappears.
a smile goes ... where? or a candid, fleeting glance—
a fresh, flushed beat freed from its heart?

that is how it is for us.
and when we have returned to stardust,
does there remain a sense of us in space?
do the angels draw in only what has emanated
from them, or sometimes, as if by mistake,
is a bit of our being caught as well?
does it alter their visages the way some women

with child seem bemused with sudden awareness
of another being within them?
or is there too much in the flurry of creation
returning to angels for them to discern our atoms?

if night could comprehend,
it might learn glorious things from lovers.
but it seems all things prefer to turn *from* us.
ancient forests still grow; old homes still stand.
only we continue travelling on, as if migrating,
while the world around us holds its breath
until we are gone, perhaps in disdain,
yet secretly curious with wonder.

i ask you lovers who cleave to each other in contentment—
who complete each other—are you sure the bond is real?
because there are times when my hands clasp themselves
in a perfect fit, or find something very special
as they hold my ordinary face, that i feel a bit more
invigorated—but who could be satisfied forever,
only with that?

you, so overcome from the building delight of the other
that you beg *no more*. ... who in each other's hands grow lush
like the harvests of vintage years, who might abandon yourselves
as the other takes you completely—would that truly be enough?
there is such pleasure, such lingering tenderness
in your touches, the places they so lovingly cover
will remember them always. such embraces, such touches
bring an attentiveness so complete that, surely,
it will last for eternity!

yet, once beyond the riveting first glances and the pining
at the window and the first stroll together in the garden—
does it still feel the same? when your lips meet,
sip by sip, is the ardor still quenched? or even there?

the ancients were more subdued. the greeks
left us statues graced with the modesty of gestures,
affection and parting resting lightly on their shoulders.
torsos straight and sound, hands held loosely.
this is how we are, they told us, this is how we touch.
gods might force themselves on us,
but that is not our way.

we search for just such a pure, reserved strain of humanity,
and a stretch of fertile cropland between river and rock,
a place where our hearts can rise above us, as did theirs.
not a place to adore with the eye or appease with the spirit,
but a place that simply lifts our hearts, high.

under his heavy lids, the sweetness of your image
glowed softly like a beacon through fog.

from *the third*

the third

is it the lover we honor,
or a deep, wanton lord of our blood?
can a young man discern delight
for his beloved from the roughened lust
that masters him, leads him in erotic frenzy
through the night? and after the chaos of desire,
listen how the night becomes so still, fathomless,
and there is endless joy in adoring a beloved's face,
radiant from the light of stars within her.

who lifts this young man's brow in questioning,
in expectation? not you, dear girl (and never mother).
his lips stir, but not with desire for yours.
your tentative touch is not what unsettles him so.
you, as drifting and amorphous as a morning breeze?
no. your femaleness may fluster his heart,
but older fears overtake him at your touch.
your clear, loving voice will not summon him
completely from those deep-rooted mysteries.
yes, he is desperate to be free of them and,
when he succeeds, finds in your safe heart
his true self. but was he the maker of that self?

it was *you* who began him, mother.
he was your tiny, fresh creation,
and you let only the world's kindnesses
bow over and be seen by those soft, new eyes.
you kept at bay the dark unknown.
where have they gone, all the years
when your slender shadow would come
quickly to calm confusion in the dark?
you hid so much from him then.
you revealed as harmless the room's
imagined monsters, and joined
the complete shelter of your heart with night,
pledging your soft aura as if in friendship.

you explained every creak, every floorboard's settling.
he hung on your every word and was comforted.
you came with such tenderness, such sureness
that looming fate retreated behind the bureau
and restless future, so easily postponed,

settled in heavy folds of the curtains.
and his own self came to rest, relieved.
under his heavy lids, the sweetness of your image
glowed softly like a beacon through fog.

but *within* him?
who controlled, checked the surges of procreation?
no one. there *was* no caution in the one asleep.
a sleep roiling with fantasies, with fevers.
it was to them he let himself be vulnerable.
to the unstoppable taproots of metamorphosis,
already wound into helixes, into dense thickets,
alive with carnal, stalking forms.
naïve, afraid, how entangled he became,
and so willingly, eagerly succumbed.

he loved this different inner man, his inner wilderness,
the private, quiet forest where his heart ripened.
he ventured deeper, beneath his roots into the vastness
of creation, where his insignificant birth already was forgotten.
yet he descended on, into the veins and vessels
of ancient canyons where the predators dwell,
still full from his forebears. there, foreboding
knew him and slyly winked in understanding.
yes, terrors smiled and, as if in reflex
he warmed to what smiled at him.
mother, do you know how rarely you smiled
with such tenderness? perhaps *before* you
this had been his comfort, already thriving
in the embryonic waters that upheld him.

you see, sweet girl, men do not love
like a flower that lives for one year.
with you in our arms, an ancient sap rises
from earth grown fertile with our fathers' dust,
from the memory of our mothers' flow in dried arroyos,
from the silent spinning of our earth in sunlight or clouds.
our love issues from what came before us.

yet understand it was your coaxing, girl,
that roused these ancient histories in your lover.
and for you, what senses churned through to you
from forgotten beings? were there women
who resented you? did you quicken the blood

of forsaken men in your young man's veins?
did children long gone yearn to be re-borne by you?
you, who so tenderly take his hand in love
and guide him toward the garden,
be his rock, be what prevails in his nights,
be his tether.

when winter begins, we and trees
that still are green have missed
the prodding to migrate or grow dormant.

from *the fourth*

the fourth

when winter begins, we and trees
that still are green have missed
the prodding to migrate or grow dormant.
like flocks passed by, aware too late,
we veer suddenly into the wind
and tumble to a cold pond. and so
we learn what it is to flower
and what it is to wither
while, in their wild lands,
lions reign with no thought to season
or future or past, and never falter.

our self-assurance, though, wavers.
the moment we pledge our hearts to one,
we hesitate, fearing we have lost another.
conflict within becomes our companion.
don't lovers shun possessiveness?
grant each other space and a haven?
yet, with each act of love,
we breach these boundaries.
we grow aware of a moment
as it is formed by events that surround it,
that hold it up for us to contemplate.
we come to know an emotion only
from acts that engage us,
like white space in a painting,
that becomes a cloud molded
by the sky that surrounds it.
your heart is anxious for the play to begin.
the curtain parts, and there is the familiar garden,
untended, and here comes … just *a* dancer, not *the*.
yes, his performance is flawless, but an act,
and when it is over, he returns home
through the kitchen door, like any of us.
and you say, *enough*! the true puppet
is what you need to see, not its costume.
the marionette who becomes alive
despite his wood and skins and strings.
you stay. wait. even as the stage
empties and the theater grows dark.
even as its emptiness settles on you,
and the lineage that brought your heart

to this place drifts away, you watch
for what you know is there.
you, father, i know you understand.
you tasted the first clouded brewing of my need,
then, sampling its bitterness again and again as I grew,
grew troubled by the aftertaste of so peculiar a future,
you pondered it as i gazed up at you.
even dead, father, your perplexity and dread
are alive within me, within my hope.
you surrender realms of lifeless rest
in worry over my fragment of fate.
and i know *you* understand, those who were smitten
at the first flicker of my feelings for you—the feelings
i always turned from as your tender openness
changed, while i loved it, into an open field
where you were no longer. …

for my attention to linger,
an angel must possess a marionette
and make their skins perform.
then at last there is a play!
a script, an actor, an angel *unite*,
and so begins an evolution, a crossing over
from stage, from imagination,
to what lives and is true. as those dying
watch the angel perform above us,
are they meant to see success
as nothing but illusion? to see
that what *is* must be something else?
when we were children, behind us
was eternity, and we did not consider
what was to come. but we grew,
could not avoid it, yet each holds close
our specialness that makes its home
in that land between world and toy.
it is a gift to lay before a child their freedom
to *be* and choose, to offer them the stars
and the means to gauge their vastness.
but to chart their course and lay the map
before them is as much a death
as abandoning in their round,
red mouth a crust of moldy bread
as if it were the heart of an apple.
we have no words for so mortal a sin.

these nomads, a bit more fugitive than ourselves,
these acrobats plied like puppets by a hidden tormenter
. . . down they come
onto a patch of home covering the ground,
a carpet worn thin from infinite landings.

from *the fifth*

the fifth

dedicated to Frau Herta von Koenig

Pablo Picasso, *Family of Saltimbanques*
© 2023 Estate of Pablo Picasso/
Artists Rights Society (ARS), New York

these nomads, a bit more fugitive than ourselves,
these acrobats plied like puppets by a hidden tormenter—
wrung, bent, coiled, swung, hurled and snatched back
slickly, as if through greased air. down they come
onto a patch of home covering the ground,
a carpet worn thin from infinite landings.
                         in the painting, their figures form
a faint *D,* perhaps for Destiny, for fate wrestles
with even the sturdiest of us, tossing us about
the way ruler augustus the strong
would crumple pewter plates for sport.

all the while, as if they form the crux of a rose,
the troupe blooms or languishes as onlookers
come and go, like petals. the rose swells
while the pollens of novelty and skill lure an audience—
but ready smiles grow sated, wistful, and begin to drift,
petals dropping.

before us is the old strongman gone to seed,
just drumming the pace now, lost in his immense,
flaccid form that could have held two men,
one already gone, the survivor a bit deaf
and baffled in his stranded skin.

and then there is the strapping youth,
a young god fleshed out with taut muscle
and sinew. naïve, new.

and you, once like a curious plaything
for a young lament in its convalescence. …

and you who, like green fruit dropping
from this human tree of collective motion
and every season of life, land hard
a hundred times a day to collide with the grave.
there are times when, in a half-rest, a kind,
timid glance yearns to travel from you
to your indifferent mother, but stumbles
in the wilderness of your body. …

again, the old strongman beats the rhythm for your leap,
and your ever racing heart is just spared from breaking.
your soles, on fire, propel you as nimbly
as even a faint ache can press your body's tears
into your eyes. yet blindly, numbly, your smile stays. …

come, angel! gather that smile as if it were
an ephemeral bloom! protect it, preserve it
among those wild herbs whose healing powers
still are not clear to us. inscribe on its own exquisite urn:
                subrizio saltat … the tumbler's smile

and you, then, sweet girl, skipped over
by the gifts of beguilement, perhaps your ruffles
are happy to be with you? or the spring green silk
shimmers as if wanting nothing more
than to coddle your new breasts?
over the shoulders of onlookers,
we see your lovely tranquility displayed,
when needed to captivate.

        that place—on land and in my heart—
        where the tumblers fell away from each other
        like coupling animals not properly paired,
        the weights still too unwieldy, the plates
        still tottering on their sticks—
        where they were so far from knowing.

but suddenly this tiresome scenario inexplicably turns;
what has been too little becomes too much,
then settles into deft equilibrium.

and so it is, on the eternal stage of paris,
where lady death braids and coils and colors
the world's restless paths as if they were ribbons
meant for winter's threadbare cloches.

*

angel, do you know of a place, unknown to us,
where a resplendent carpet is lain for lovers
to find embraces never shared in this world?
turrets of desire built where earth does not exist,
their spiraling steps rising on each other forever,
simply, trembling in sublime climax for an audience
of innumerable, inaudible dead—
                    the voyeurs who would toss their final,
prized coin of blessing into the hat on the carpet
for these lovers, contented, quenched at last.

then, a warm night lures,
prises open lips and lids, and sighs and clear eyes
in tandem hurry toward an ecstasy of bloom . . .

from *the sixth*

the sixth

fig, your fruit is so miraculous to me—
petite, secret flowers captive within its walls
and none evading perfect pollination.
down, then upward you propel your sap,
like zeus as the swan intent on pleasure.

but we humans are diverted in our timing,
frittering away our chances while admiring
our dazzling blossom more than its singular fruit.
perhaps the gardener strung the veins differently
in some of us, buds plumping more quickly
from an impatient, inner flow. then, a warm night
lures, pries open lips and lids, and sighs and clear eyes
in tandem hurry toward an ecstasy of *bloom*
like the victor rushed onward by his stallions.

to last and grow old is unknown to such a hero,
as it is to those who die young. ascension is his calling,
driven by risk toward the flickering constellations.
you and i could not follow him there, where a fate
we know nothing of greets him, bears him home
with the joy of a father finding his prodigal son.
we so barely discern this ecstasy, so briefly reel
from its swift, fleeting passage through us.

how the boy in me longed to be like samson,
whose mother first bore nothing, then so much.
within you, mother, already he was heroic.
from thousands vying for the prize in your womb,
he clearly prevailed, then broke from your belly
to shatter the chains and pillars of yet another world.
mothers of heroes, your wombs give refuge
to these turbulent streams, into whose eroded ravines
young women fall from high ledges, heartbroken,
like offerings destined for your sons.

every heartbeat that loves him
spurs a hero beyond himself, beyond his smile,
prodding him through the binding spells of love
to the strange terrain of the land of transformation.

those springtimes understood, carried your clear call
to every corner, and dormant things began to open . . .

from *the seventh*

the seventh

gone, my voice, are your seasons of bold seduction,
those early springs when you crooned and trilled
as brightly as a fertile bird roused from solitude
to sing its mate into the radiance of sky.
like his, voice, you stirred a quiet friend
still hidden among new leaves, watching,
then warming, kindling, burning with your fervor.

those springtimes understood, carried your clear call
to every corner, and dormant things began to open,
lifted themselves to the peace of early sunlight,
to the muffled tones of a familiar, unruffled day.
as if a spell were broken, then, as if a neglected temple,
silent and overgrown, were rediscovered, the stilled streams
beneath it found their flow again and burst their song
through the dried fountains, summoning brilliant summer
before the ebb to autumn.

each day of summer answers—with each glistening daybreak,
each flicker of light on every vibrant flower, each lingering glance
through vast canopies of trees, the summer days unfold like paths
before us, like fields rippling toward their dusk horizon.
and then the summer nights—that take away the sun
yet leave behind the other stars, so distant now but not forever.
until we die and join them, we will love their light from here.

like the insistent bird, i had called to my lover, but with her
came others, maidens risen from the makeshift graves
i had given them—those who have merged with earth
still quicken at its springtime call,
for anything felt deeply here is not forgotten.
and as you maidens overtake your lovers,
it is the giddy race from childhood that brings you,
breath after breath, from nowhere into everywhere.

we are so blessed to be here!
even young women understood, those stranded
in city streets that stank like open sores.
each woman there knew respites, the spans of time
between two moments when they *bloomed*
and light filled every vein. to others,
that kind of joy might not be envied, not admired,

because it cannot be displayed for all to see.
but when held close within us, it transfigures.

our world exists, my love, within us only.
we adjust, we adapt, always evolving
toward thriving in the frontier within us.
a house once sturdy might now be gone,
yet the home itself glows in our minds,
reimagined and restored, eternal.
now, the soul of our age hoards *power,*
an amorphous treasure stockpiled in secret,
as if defiling sacred spaces.
yet such temples do still stand holy
in some of us—*in* us their arches soar
and impossible columns rise to heaven.

each listless turning of earth casts off those
who own no past and will not know a future—
for whom even the next second can be too distant.
rather than sadden us, it should affirm our task
of keeping safe the ruins of symbols sacred
to those who once stood in power among us,
uncertain of their destiny, yet able to touch the stars.
angel, it is for *your* eyes—there! In your sight
the pillars stand whole and upright, open and eternal,
even among the lost cities of their followers.

and we *did* preserve the holy—a miracle, yes?
to think that truly we have kept these spaces of ours
enduring. the soaring cathedrals we built—and *music,*
reaching higher still, even beside *you*, angel!
even one lover, alone by her window at night …
even *she* came up to your mighty knee!
        no, angel,
i do not presume we are equal,
or even that you might see me here, but my calls
to you always are coming and departing,
like currents holding you in place.
although faint, my voice, inconceivable one,
is like an outstretched arm
whose hand stays open before you
as my shield and my warning.

we do not see the clearing in the wilderness,
nor breathe in its sweet air. it is the place
where children live and are called back from.

from *the eighth*

the eighth

dedicated to Rudolf Kastner

open spaces have no boundaries
in the sweeping eyes of animals.
only our eyes glance back uncertainly,
as if to hold the limitless in place.
even our children learn to turn back,
to censor *possibility* from *future*.
an animal might pause at our hesitancy
yet quickly resume its rustling flow
in the infinite frontier it passes through.
               never do *we* have in our sights
the expanse that blooms and swells forever,
but rather the finite world of longing, of *no*.

we do not see the clearing in the wilderness,
nor breathe in its sweet air. it is the place
where children live and are called back from.
it is what those near death begin to see,
and become, as they lose sight of earth.
one lover draws near in amazement,
the other blocks their view as again and again
the clearing flickers between them until overgrown.
as if in a mirror we see the natural world around us,
our own reflection eclipsing the view,
and we know the world from the eyes of animals
as they gaze at us, and into us, and through us.
that is our destiny: to know of the wondrous
and be in awe, but never to enter it and *become*.
if the nimble beast moving toward us
lived by thoughts like ours, such a being
would drive us to extinction. but the animal
lives outside of existence or meaning or fate.
it simply *is*, and always has been, always will be.

and yet, this creature pulls a burden as it moves,
a deep sorrow of the memory that once we neared
mysteries together, with exquisite tenderness.
but here, with our first cry of breath in the world,
we became separate; there, we breathed together.

look at the little being that never leaves its womb—
a fly still soars inside it, even to mate, because *womb*

is all around. and a bird—sealed in an egg
like an etruscan in his crypt, under a resting likeness—
in a startled rush it shatters its home,
like a bat cleaving a flawless evening sky.

a sky we are watching always,
because always we are spectators.
always looking *at*, never *away*.
what we see might overwhelm us,
and so we alter it, and nearly lose it.
we grasp it, alter it again, and lose ourselves.

and always we seem to be leaving.
why? who has made us this way?
there, on a last hill, all that we have lived
lies behind and below us,
and always we linger, turning to take it in
and turning again to leave it.

with just one springtime
we understand transformation,
the sacred mission of earth to dissolve
completely into each of us …

from *the ninth*

the ninth

why stay human
if we could switch at will into a laurel,
evergreen, with the deepest, richest leaves
waving like open hands to all around it?
we sentient beings who spurn,
yet yearn for, our destiny?
        we do stay human,
but not because of happiness,
which seems to decay into loss,
nor to humor curiosity,
or to strengthen spirit.

we stay for our sole performance,
in a role meant for no one else.
one time for everything of this world
everywhere in it, only *once* and no more,
and for us, too, *one* time.
all that is in earth and on it
and each transit of time needs to touch us,
and us to touch it, as if to assure ourselves
that we *are* now and once *were*.

we long to receive-open-become all of it,
this gift of lifetime continually unfolding
in our simple hands, fascinating to our eyes,
incredible beyond words to our hearts.
and when it is ours fully, what then?
do we in turn gift it, or take it with us?
what of us *here* travels with us beyond death,
and what remains? perception, so carefully learned,
will stay behind. all that has occurred here will stay.
sorrows, then, or trials, or the deep study of love
and, on its heels, the surprise of the genuine,
inexpressible even under starlight.

        it is the gentian from the mountainside,
        the blue and yellow poem of sky and sun,
        that the hiker gathers, not its hidden soil.

and in our time here, perhaps we leave
our imprint on *house, bridge, well, gate,*
pitcher, fruit tree, window, pillar, tower.

it is day by night that lovers wear down
their doorstep, as did the many before them,
as will the many after.

like a chick splits its shell,
what the living outgrow falls away,
begetting different borders to test.
here, we are in the time and home
of all that is *spoken*, and the spoken
is what we *know*. even if we stammer,
our hammering heart endures
and our tongue knows only praise.

with our angel, we share this praise, grateful
for the world and what we have wrought in it,
not to impress, but to tell the simple stories
of how we leave our mark here,
of what those before us left behind,
of what we leave for others to come.
to the angel in its heavens, flourishing
like a green bay tree, we are barely saplings,
yet he will stand in awe of our earthly artifacts,
of their pureness and the delight they bring,
of how even pain resolves to take a shape,
serve in some way, or perish in some thing,
the way a violin's mournful sound flies off
and dies away beyond it. we mortals cherish all
that lives on as it leaves the world and vanishes
into us, transfigured again and again into stardust.

isn't there, at earth's core, a magnetic heart
compelling separate bodies into one,
kindling all that is? with just one springtime
we understand transformation,
the sacred mission of earth to dissolve
completely into each of us, to be devoted
to a final rest inside us.

together, as this hybrid being,
we have traveled what seems forever,
without horizons, neither childhood
nor future diminishing, yet with a fertile heart
heavy with the life remaining.

catkins hanging from their leafless hazel tree,
or rain falling on the dark sprngtime earth—
are these our analogies for the eternal dead?

from *the tenth*

the tenth

and when this relentless regimen
of enlightenment comes to its close,
i will be radiant, my face streaming
with simple weeping as i bring my joy
to kindred angels. none of the notes
of my heart will fail, and i will hold
dearer those sorrows i wore
like winter foliage, evergreen—
those sisters of grief i did not yield to,
inconsolable sirens whose loosened hair
was never gathered in my hands,
whose duration and uncertain end
became my wasted worry.

despair lives for just one season
of our stay here, in just one of many houses.
but to a youth, it is an unfamiliar city,
full of white noise from steady bedlam,
where the gaudy offspring of inanity swaggers
and staggers like a fractured shrine collapsing.
any angel would trample to dust such a city,
scatter to oblivion its markets,
flatten its manufactured churches,
tidy and shut.
                  but the city limits
still bristle with festival! for the youth,
there are swings, jugglers, shooting galleries
where one good hit fells every target!
through applause and chance he wanders on.
even for those older, there is a special display:
the anatomical, private parts of money—
having sex, proliferating! performing
the pornography of wealth begetting wealth.
at the city's outskirts awaits the final distraction,
the promise of eternal life, *no death*!
but the youth looks beyond the outskirts
toward what is more familiar—
children at play, lovers in the patchy grass,
dogs marking territory. and still
the youth ventures on, trailing a maiden lament,
perhaps, as she enters the outer meadows.
far off, she tells him, *we live out there*.

and he gazes, wondering *where*?
he is smitten by her beauty, her bearing—
but she is so different. he turns to go,
and turns back, uncertain.

only the fledgling dead, still being weaned
toward a peace with no beginning, no end,
follow her sweetly. she takes the maidens
under her wing, gently showing them
her lustrous pearls of affliction,
her exquisite veils of endurance.
but with the young men, she is quiet.

there, in their valley of laments,
an elder warms to the questioning youth.
once, she tells him, *we laments were a great race,*
with great wealth. our forebears mined
those mountains. among men, you might see
a polished ingot of primal pain, or obsidian
from a snuffed volcano—yes, our artifacts.

and through the vast lands of lamentation,
she guides the youth. through the temple pillars
and ruins of the citadels where princes of lament
ruled wisely. under the shade of the lofty trees of tears.
he is awed by prairies blooming with wild melancholy,
by the nimble, grazing deer of mourning.
a startled bird suddenly flies through their line of sight,
its flight filling the sky with the language of its desolate cry.
at dusk, the elder and youth pass by the ancient tombs
of sybils and diviners but, as darkness falls,
a sepulcher rises before them like a moon.
they marvel at the face of the sealed crypt,
so like the sphinx—the face of man, the crowned head
that has been set forever, silent, on the scale of the stars.

it is too vast for the youth to see completely,
but not for the elder, whose gaze startles an owl
behind the crown. though it coasts down in quiet
along the fullest curve of cheek, the youth hears
its wings lightly brush the enigmatic contour,
so like an opened book with a tale to tell.

and higher still, *stars*. new stars,
seen only from the land of despair.
there is the horseman, points the elder, *and the staff,*
and the bountiful garland of fruit. again she points,
look there, toward the pole—*there is the cradle, the path,*
the burning book, the puppet, the window.
but in the southern sky, clear and brilliant,
stands the *m* for *mother.* ...

he yearns to see more, the youth,
and under the silent moon, the elder brings him
to *the gorge.* there, at the foot of the mountains,
the glistening *spring of joy* bubbles and flows,
a sustaining river to the living. overcome,
weeping, she embraces him. he is here to climb
the mountains, to pay homage to their primal pain,
yet the scuffling of each step
is muffled by the soundless slopes.

*

catkins *hanging* from their leafless hazel tree,
or rain *dropping* on the dark springtime earth—
are these our analogies for the eternal dead?

will we, whose happiness now *lifts* us,
bear it when happiness *falls*?

Duineser Elegien
Rainer Maria Rilke

Aus dem Besitz der Fürstin
Marie von Thurn und Taxis-Hohenlohe

Die Erste Elegie

Wer, wenn ich schriee, hörte mich denn aus der Engel
Ordnungen? und gesetzt selbst, es nähme
einer mich plötzlich ans Herz; ich verginge von seinem
stärkeren Dasein. Denn das Schöne ist nichts
als den Schrecklichen Anfang, den wir noch grade ertragen,
und wir berundern es so, weil es gelassen verschmäht,
und zu zerstören. Ein jeder Engel is schrecklich.
Und so verhalt ich mich denn und verschlucke den Lockruf
dunkelen Schluchzens. Ach, wen vermögen
wir denn zu brauchen? Engel nicht, Menschen nicht,
und die findigen Tiere merken es schon,
daß wir nicht sehr verläßlich zu Haus sind
in der gedeuteten Welt. Es bleibt uns vielleicht
irgend ein Baum an dem Abhang, daß wir ihn täglich
wiedersähen; es bleibt uns die Straße von gestern
und das verzogene Treusein einer Gewohnheit,
der es bei uns gefiel, und so blieb sie und ging nicht.
    O und die Nacht, die Nacht, wenn der Wind voller Weltraum
uns am Angesicht zehrt—, wem bliebe sie nicht, die ersehnte,
sanft entiäuschende, welche dem einzelnen Herzen
mühsam bevorsteht. Ist sie den Liebended leichter?
Ach, sie verdecken sich nur mit einander ihr Los.
    Weißt du's *noch* nicht? Wirf aus den Armen die Leere
zu den Räumen hinzu, die wir atmen; vielleicht daß die Vögel
die erweiterte Luft fühlen mit innigerm Flug.

Ja, die Frühlinge brauchten dich wohl. Es muteten manche
Sterne dir zu, daß du sie spürtest. Es hob
sich eine Woge heran im Vergangenen, oder
da du vorüberkamst am geöffneten Fenster,
gab eine Geige sich hin. Das alles war Auftrag.

Ja, die Frühlinge brauchten dich wohl. Es muteten manche
Sterne dir zu, daß du sie spürtest. Es hob
sich eine Woge heran im Vergangenen, oder .
da du vorüberkamst am geöffneten Fenster,
gab eine Geige sich hin. Das alles war Auftrag.
Aber bewältigtest du's? Warst du nicht immer
noch von Erwartung zerstreut, als kündigte alles
eine Geliebte dir an? (Wo willst du sie bergen,
da doch die großen fremden Gedanken bei dir
aus und ein gehn und öfters bleiben bei Nacht.)

Sehnt es dich aber, so singe die Liebenden; lange
noch nicht unsterblich genug ist ihr berühmtes Gefühl.
Jene, du neidest sie fast, Verlassenen, die du
so viel liebender fandst als die Gestillten. Beginn
immer von neuem die nie zu erreichende Preisung;
denk: es erhält sich der Held, selbst der Untergang war ihm
nur ein Vorwand, zu sein: seine letzte Geburt.
Aber die Liebenden nimmt die erschöpft Natur
in sich zurück, als wären nicht zweimal die Kräfte,
dieses zu leisten. Hast due der Gaspara Stampa
denn genügend gedacht, daß irgend ein Mädchen,
dem der Geliebte entging, am gesteigerten Beispiel
dieser Liebenden fühlt: daß ich würde wie sie?
Sollen nicht endlich uns diese ältesten Schmerzen
fruchtbarer werden? Ist es nicht Zeit, daß wir liebend
uns vom Geliebten befrein und es bebend bestehn:
wie der Pfeil die Sehne besteht, um gesammelt im Absprung
mehr zu sein als er selbst. Denn Bleiben ist nirgends.

Stimmen, Stimmen. Höre, mein Herz, wie sonst nur
Heilige hörten: daß sie der riesige Ruf
aufhob vom Boden; sie aber knieten,
Unmög1iche, weiter und achtetens nicht:
So waren sie hörend. Nicht, daß du *Gottes* ertrügest
die Stimme, bei weitem. Aber das Wehende höre,
die ununterbrochene Nachricht, die aus Stille sich bildet.
Es rauscht jetzt von jenen jungen Toten zu dir.
Wo immer du eintratst, redete nicht in Kirchen
zu Rom und Neapel ruhig ihr Schicksal dich an?
Oder es trug eine Inschrift sich erhaben dir auf,
wie neulich die Tafel in Santa Maria Formosa.
Was sie mir wollen? leise soll ich des Unrechts
Anschein abtun, der ihrer Geister
reine Bewegung manchmal ein wenig behindert.

Freilich ist es seltsam, die Erde nicht mehr zu bewohnen,
kaum erlen te Gebräuche nicht mehr zu üben,
Rosen, und andern eigens versprechenden Dingen
nicht die Bedeutung menschlicher Zukunft zu geben;
das, was man war in unendlich ängstlichen Händen,
nicht mehr zu sein, und selbst den eigenen Narnen
wegzulassen wie ein zerbrochenes Spielzeug.
Seltsam, die Wünsche nicht weiterzuwünschen. Seltsam,
alles, was sich bezog, so lose im Raume

flattern zu sehen. Und das Totsein ist mühsam
und voller Nachholn, daß man allmählich ein wenig
Ewigkeit spürt. —Aber Lebendige machen
alle den Fehler, daß sie zu stark unterscheiden.
Engel (sagt man) wüßten oft nicht, ob sie unter
Lebenden gehn oder Toten. Die ewige Strömung
reißt durch beide Bereiche alle Alter
immer mit sich und übertönt sie in beiden.

Schließich brauchen sie uns nicht mehr, die Früheentrückten,
man entwöhnt sich des Irdischen sanft, wie man den Brüsten
milde der Mutter entwächst. Aber wir, die so große
Geheimnisse brauchen, denen aus Trauer so oft
seliger Fortschritt entspringt—: *könntcn* wir sein ohne sie?

Ist die Sage umsonst, daB einst in der Klage um Linos
wagende erste Musik dürre Erstarrung durchdrang;
daß erst im erschrockenen Raum, dem ein beinah göttlicher
Jüngling plötzlich für immer enttrat, das Leere in jene
Schwingung geriet, die uns jetzt hinreißt und tröstet und hilft.

Die Zweite Elegie

Jeder Engel ist schrecklich. Und dennoch, weh mir,
ansing ich euch, fast tödliche Vögel der Seele,
wissend um euch. Wohin sind die Tage Tobiae,
da der Strahlendsten einer stand an der einfachen Haustür,
zur Reise ein wenig verkleidet und schon nicht mehr furchtbar;
(Jüngling dem Jüngling, wie er neugierig hinaussah).
Träte der Erzengel jetzt, der gefährliche, hinter den Sternen
eines Schrittes nur nieder und herwärts: hochauf-
schlagend erschlug uns das eigene Herz. Wer seid ihr?

Frühe Geglückte, ihr Verwöhnten der Schöpfung,
Höhenzüge, morgenrötliche Grate
aller Erschaffung,—Pollen der bluhenden Gottheit,
Gelenke des Lichtes, Gänge, Treppen, Throne,
Räume aus Wesen, Schilde aus Wonne, Tumulte
stürmisch entzückten Gefühls und plötzlich, einzeln,
Spiegel: die die enströrnte eigene Schönheit
wiederschöpfen zurück in das eigene Antlitz.

Denn wir, wo wir fühlen, verflüchtigen; ach wir
atmen uns aus und dahin; von Holzglut zu Holzglut
geben wir schwächern Geruch. Da sagt uns wohl einer:
ja, du gehst mir ins Blut, dieses Zimmer, der Frühling
füllt sich mit dir … Was hilfts, er kann uns nicht halten,
wir schwinden in ihm und um ihn. Und jene, die schön sind,
o wer hält sie zurück? Unaufhörlich steht Anschein
auf in ihrem Gesicht und geht fort. Wie Tau von dem Frühgras
hebt sich das Unsre von uns, wie die Hitze von einem
heißen Gericht. O Lächeln, wohin? O Aufschaun:
neue, warme, entgehende Welle des Herzens—;
weh mir: wir *sinds* doch. Schmeckt denn der Weltraum,
in den wir uns lösen, nach uns? Fangen die Engel
wirklich nur Ihriges auf, ihnen Entströmtes,
oder ist manchmal, wie aus Versehen, ein wenig
unseres Wesens dabei? Sind wir in ihre
Züge soviel nur gemischt wie das Vage in die Gesichter
schwangerer Frauen? Sie merken es nicht in dem Wirbel
ihrer Rückkehr zu sich. (Wie sollten sie's merken.)

Liebende könnten, verstünden sie's, in der Nachtluft
wunderlich reden. Denn es scheint, daß uns alles
verheimlicht. Siehe, die Bäume *sind*; die Häuser,

die wir bewohnen, bestehn noch. Wir nur
ziehen allem vorbei wie ein luftiger Austausch.
Und alles ist einig, uns zu verschweigen, halb als
Schande vielleicht und halb als unsägliche Hoffnung.

Liebende, euch, ihr in einander Genügten,
frag ich nach uns. Ihr greift euch. Habt ihr Beweise?
Seht, mir geschiehts, daß meine Hände einander
inne werden oder daB mein gebrauchtes
Gesicht in ihnen sich schont. Das giebt mir ein wenig
Empfindung. Doch wer wagte darum schon zu *sein*?
Ihr aber, die ihr im Entzücken des anderen
zunehmt, bis er euch überwältigt
anflecht: nicht *mehr*—; die ihr unter den Händen
euch reichlicher werdet wie Traubenjahre;
die ihr manchmal vergeht, nur weil der andre
ganz überhand nimmt: euch frag ich nach uns. Ich weiß,
ihr berührt euch so selig, weil die Liebkosung verhält,
weil die Stelle nicht schwindet, die ihr, Zärtliche,
zudeckt; weil ihr darunter das reine
Dauern verspürt. So versprecht ihr euch Ewigkeit fast
von der Umarmung. Und doch, wenn ihr der ersten
Blicke Schrecken besteht und die Sehnsucht am Fenster,
und den ersten gemeinsamen Gang, *ein* Mal durch den Garten:
Liebende, *seid* ihrs dann noch? Wenn ihr einer dem andern
euch an den Mund hebt und ansetzt—: Getränk an Getränk:
o wie entgeht dann der Trinkende seltsam der Handlung.

Erstaunte euch nicht auf attischen Stelen die Vorsicht
menschlicher Geste? war nicht Liebe und Abschied
so leicht auf die Schultern gelegt, als war es aus anderm
Stoffe gemacht als bei uns? Gedenkt euch der Hände,
wie sie drucklos beruhen, obwohl in den Tor sen die Kraft steht.
Diese Beherrschten wußten damit: so weit sind wirs,
dieses unser, uns *so* zu berühren; stärker
stemmen die Götter uns an. Doch dies ist Sache der Götter.

Fänden auch wir ein reines, verhaltenes, schmales
Menschliches, einen unseren Streifen Fruchtlands
zwischen Strom und Gestein. Denn das eigene Herz übersteigt
uns noch immer wie jene. Und wir können ihm nicht mehr
nachschaun in Bilder, die es besänftigen, noch in
göttliche Körper, in denen es größer sich mäßigt.

Die Dritte Elegie

Eines ist, die Geliebte zu singen. Ein anderes, wehe,
jenen verborgenen schuldigen Fluß-Gott des Bluts.
Den sie von weitem erkennt, ihren Jüngling, was weiß er
selbst von dem Herren der Lust, der aus dem Einsamen oft,
ehe das Mädchen noch linderte, oft auch als wäre sie nicht,
ach, von welchem Unkenntlichen triefend, das Gotthaupt
aufhob, aufrufend die Nacht zu unendlichem Aufruhr.
O des Blutes Neptun, o sein furchtbarer Dreizack.
O der dunkele Wind seiner Brust aus gewundener Muschel.
Horch, wie die Nacht sich mulder und höhlt. Ihr Sterne,
stammt nicht von euch des Liebenden Lust zu dem Antlitz
seiner Geliebten? Hat er die innige Einsicht
in ihr reines Gesicht nicht aus dem reinen Gestirn?

Du nicht hast ihm, wehe, nicht seine Mutter
hat ihm die Bogen der Braun so zur Erwartung gespannt.
Nicht an dir, ihn fühlendes Mädchen, an dir nicht
bog seine Lippe sich zum fruchtbarern Ausdruck.
Meinst du wirklich, ihn hatte dein leichter Auftritt
also erschüttert, du die wandelt wie Frühwind?
Zwar du erschrakst ihm das Herz; doch ältere Schrecken
stürzten in ihn bei dem berührenden Anstoß.
Ruf ihn ... du ruft st ihn nicht ganz aus dunkelem Umgang.
Freilich, er *will*, er entspringt; erleichtert gewöhnt er
sich in dein heimliches Herz und nimmt und beginnt sich.
Aber begann er sich je?
Mutter, *du* machtest ihn klein, du warsts, die ihn anfing;
dir war er neu, du beugtest über die neuen
Augen die freundliche Welt und wehrtest der fremden.
Wo, ach, hin sind die Jahre, da du ihm einfach
mit der schlanken Gestalt wallendes Chaos vertratst?
Vieles verbargst du ihm so; das nächtlich-verdächtige Zimmer
machtest du harmlos, aus deinem Herzen voll Zuflucht
mischtest du menschlichern Raum seinem Nacht-Raum hinzu.
Nicht in die Finsternis, nein, in dein näheres Dasein hast du
das Nachtlicht gestellt, und es schien wie aus Freundschaft.
Nirgends ein Knistern, das du nicht lächelnd erklärtest,
so al wüßtest du längst, *wann* sich die Diele benimmt ...
Und er horchte und linderte sich. So vieles vermochte
zärtlich dein Aufstehn; hinter den Schrank trat
hoch im Mantel sein Schicksal, und in die Falten des Vorhangs
paßte, die leicht sich verschob, seine unruhige Zukunft.

Und er selbst, wie er lag, der Erleichterte, unter
schläfernden Lidern deiner leichten Gestaltung
Süße lösend in den gekosteten Vorschlaf—:
schien ein Gehüteter ... Aber *innen*: wer wehrte,
hinderte innen in ihm die Fluten der Herkunft?
Ach, da *war* keine Vorsicht im Schlafenden; schlafend,
aber träumend, aber in Fiebern: wie er sich ein-ließ.
Er, der Neue, Scheuende, wie er verstrickt war,
mit des innern Geschehns weiterschlagenden Ranken
schon zu Mustern verschlungen, zu würgendem Wachstum,
zu tierhaft jagenden Formen. Wie er sich hingab—. Liebte.
Liebte sein Inneres, seines inneren Wildnis,
diesen Urward in ihm auf dessen stummem Gesturztsein
lichtgrün sein Herz stand. Liebte. Verließ es, ging die
eigenen Wurzeln hinaus in gewaltigen Ursprung,
wo seine kleine Geburt schon überlebt war. Liebend
stieg er hinab in das ältere Blut, in die Schluchten,
wo das Furchtbare lag, noch satt von den Vätern. Und jedes
Schreckliche kannte ihn, blinzelte, war wir verständigt.
Ja, das Entsetzliche lächelte ... Selten
has du so zärtlich gelächelt, Mutter. Wie sollte
er es nicht lieben, da es ihm lächelte. *Vor* dir
hat ers geliebt, denn, da du ihn trugst schon,
war es im Wasser gelöst, das den Keimenden leicht macht.

Siehe, wir lieben nicht, wie die Blumen, aus einem
einzigen Jahr; uns steigt, wo wir lieben,
unvordenklicher Saft in die Arme. O Mädchen,
dies: daß wir liebten *in* uns, nicht Eines, ein Künftiges, sondern
das zahllos Brauende; nicht ein einzelnes Kind,
sondern die Väter, die wie Trümmer Gebirgs
uns im Grunde beruhn; sondern das trockene Flußbett
einstiger Mütter—: sondern die ganze
lautlose Landschaft unter dem wolkigen oder
reinen Verhängnis—: *dies* kam dir, Mädchen, zuvor.

Und du selber, was weißt du— du locktest
Vorzeit empor in dem Liebenden. Welche Gefühle
wühlten herauf aus entwandelten Wesen. Welche
Frauen haßten dich da. Wasfür finstere Männer
regtest du auf im Geäder des Jünglings? Tote
Kinder wollten zu dir ... O leise, leise,

tu ein liebes vor ihm, ein verläßliches Tagwerk,—führ ihn
nah an den Garten heran, gieb ihm der Nächte
Übergewicht ......
       Verhalt ihn ......

Die Vierte Elegie

O Bäume Lebens, o wann winterlich?
Wir sind nicht einig. Sind nicht wie die Zug-
vögel verständigt. Überholt und spat,
so drängen wir uns plötzlich Winden auf
und fallen ein auf teilnahmslosen Teich.
Blühn und verdorrn ist uns zugleich bewußt.
Und irgendwo gehn Löwen noch und wissen,
solang sie herrlich sind, von keiner Ohnmacht.

Uns aber, wo wir Eines meinen, ganz,
ist schon des andern Aufwand fühlbar. Feindschaft
ist uns das Nächste. Treten Liebende
nicht immerfort an Ränder, eins im andern,
die sich versprachen Weite, Jagd und Heimat.
Da wird für eines Augenblickes Zeichnung
ein Grund von Gegenteil bereitet, mühsam,
daß wir sie sähen; denn man ist sehr deutlich
mit uns. Wir kennen den Kontur
des Fühlens nicht: nur, was ihn formt von außen.
Wer saß nicht bang vor seines Herzens Vorhang?
Der schlug sich auf: die Szenerie war Abschied.
Leicht zu verstehen. Der bekannte Garten,
und schwankte leise: dann erst kam der Tänzer.
Nicht *der*. Genung! Und wenn er auch so leicht tut,
er ist verkleidet und er wird ein Bürger
und geht durch seine Küche in die Wohnung.
Ich will nicht diese halbgefüllten Masken,
lieber die Puppe. Die ist voll. Ich will
den Balg aushalten und den Draht und ihr
Gesicht aus Aussehn. Hier. Ich bin davor.
Wenn auch die Lampen ausgehn, wenn mir auch
gesagt wird: Nichts mehr—, wenn auch von der Bühne
das Leere herkommt mit dem grauen Luftzug,
wenn auch von meinen stillen Vorfahrn Keiner
mehr mit mir dasitzt, keine Frau, sogar
der Knabe nicht mehr mit dem braunen Schielaug:
Ich bleibe dennoch. Es giebt immer Zuschaun.

Hab ich nicht recht? Du, der um mich so bitter
das Leben schmeckte, meines kostend, Vater,
den ersten trüben Aufguß meines Müssens,
da ich heranwuchs, immer wieder kostend

und, mit dem Nachgeschmack so fremder Zukunft
beschäftigt, prüftest mein beschlagnes Aufschaun,—
der du, mein Vater, seit du tot bist, oft
in meiner Hoffnung, innen in mir, Angst hast,
und Gleichmut, wie ihn Tote haben, Reiche
von Gleichmut, aufgiebst für mein bißchen Schicksal,
hab ich nicht recht? Und ihr, hab ich nicht recht,
die ihr mich liebtet für den kleinen Anfang
Liebe zu euch, von dem ich immer abkam,
weil mir der Raum in eurem Angesicht,
da ich ihn liebte, überging in Weltraum,
in dem ihr nicht mehr wart … wenn mir zumut ist,
zu warten vor der Puppenbühne, nein,
so völlig hinzuschaun, daß, um mein Schauen
am Ende aufzuwiegen, dort als Spieler
ein Engel hinmuß, der die Bälge hochreißt.

Engel und Puppe: dann ist endlich Schauspiel.
Dann kommt zusammen, was wir immerfort
entzwein, indem wir da sind. Dann entsteht
aus unsern Jahreszeiten erst der Umkreis
des ganzen Wandelns. Über uns hinüber
spielt dann der Engel. Sieh, die Sterbenden,
sollten sie nicht vermuten, wie voll Vorwand
das alles ist, was wir hier leisten. Alles
ist nicht es selbst. O Stunden in der Kindheit,
da hinter den Figuren mehr als nur
Vergangnes war und vor uns nicht die Zukunft.
Wir wuchsen freilich und wir drängten manchmal,
bald groß zu werden, denen halb zulieb,
die andres nicht mehr hatten, als das Großsein.
Und waren doch, in unserem Alleingehn,
mit Dauerndem vergnugt und standen da
im Zwischenraurne zwischen Welt und Spielzeug,
an einer Stelle, die seit Anbeginn
gergründet war für einen reinen Vorgang.

Wer zeigt ein Kind, so wie es steht? Wer stellt
es ins Gestirn und giebt das Maß des Abstands
ihm in die Hand? Wer macht den Kindertod
aus grauem Brot, das hart wird,—oder läßt
ihn drin im runden Mund, so wie den Gröps
von einem schonen Apfel? …. Mörder sind

leicht einzusehen. Aber dies: den Tod,
den ganzen Tod, noch *vor* dem Leben so
sanft zu enthalten und nicht bös zu sein,
ist unbeschreiblich.

Die Funfte Elegie

Frau Hertha Koenig zugeeignet

We aber *sind* sie, sag mir, die Fahrenden, diese ein wenig
Flüchtigern noch als wir selbst, die dringend von früh an
wringt ein *wem—wem* zu Liebe
niemals zufriedener Wille? Sondern er wringt sie,
biegt sie, schlingt sie und schwingt sie,
wirft sie und fängt sie zurück; wie aus geölter,
glatterer Luft kommen sie nieder
auf dem verzehrten, von ihrem ewigen
Aufsprung dunneren Teppich, diesem verlorenen
Teppich im Weltall.
Aufgelegt wie ein Pflaster, als hätte der Vorstadt—
Himmel der Erde dort wehe getan.
                    Und kaum dort,
aufrecht, da und gezeigt: des Dastehns
großer Anfangsbuchstab …, schon auch, die stärksten
Männer, rollt sie wieder, zum Scherz, der immer
kommende Griff, wie August der Starke bei Tisch
einen zinnenen Teller.

Ach und um diese
Mitte, die Rose des Zuschauns:
blüht und entblättert. Um diesen
Stampfer, den Stempel, den von dem eignen
blühenden Staub getroffnen, zur Scheinfrucht
wieder der Unlust befruchteten, ihrer
niemals bewußten,—glänzend mit dünnster
Oberfläche leicht scheinlächelnden Unlust.

Da: der welke, faltige Stemmer,
der alte, der nur noch trommelt,
eingegangen in seiner gewaltigen Haut, als hätte sie früher
zwei Männer enthalten, und einer
läge nun schon auf dem Kirchlof, und er überlebte den andern,
taub und manchmal ein wenig
wirr, in der verwitweten Haut.

Aber der junge, der Mann, als wär er der Sohn eines Nackens
und einer Nonne: prall und strammig erfüllt
mit Muskeln und Einfalt.

Oh ihr,
die ein Leid, das noch klein war,
einst als Spielzeug bekam, in einer seiner
langen Genesungen .....
Du, der mit dem Aufschlag,
wie nur Früchte ihn kennen, unreif,
täglich hundert Mal abfällt vom Baum der gemeinsam
erbauten Bewegung (der, rascher als Wasser, in wenig
Minuten Lenz, Sommer und Herbst hat) —
abfällt und anprallt ans Grab:
manchmal, in halber Pause, will dir ein liebes
Antlitz entstehn hinüber zu deiner selten
zärtlichen Mutter; doch an deinen Körper verliert sich,
der es flächig verbraucht, das schüchtern
kaum versuchte Gesicht ... Und wieder
klatscht der Mann in die Hand zu dem Ansprung, und eh dir
jemals ein Schmerz deutlicher. wird in der Nähe des immer
trabenden Herzens, kommt das Brennen der Fußsohln
ihm, seinem Ursprung, zuvor mit ein paar dir
rasch in die Augen gejagten leiblichen Tränen.
Und dennoch, blindlings,
das Lächeln .....

Engel! o nimms, pflücks, das kleinblütige Heilkraut.
Schaff eine Vase, verwahrs! Stells unter jene, uns *noch* nicht
offenen Freuden; in lieblicher Urne
ruhms mit blumiger schwungiger Aufschrift:

« Subrisio Saltat »

Du dann, Liebliche,
du, von den reizendsten Freuden
stumm Übersprungne. Vielleicht sind
deine Fransen glücklich für dich— ,
oder über den jungen
prallen Brüsten die grüne metallene Seide
fühlt sich unendlich verwöhnt und entbehrt nichts.
Du,
immerfort anders auf alle des Gleichgewichts
schwankende Waagen
hingelegt Marktfrucht des Gleichmuts,
öffentlich unter den Schultern.

Wo, o *wo* ist der Ort—ich trag ihn im Herzen—,
wo sie noch lange nicht *konnten*, noch von einander

63

abfieln, wie sich bespringende, nicht recht
paarige Tiere;—
wo die Gewichte noch schwer sind;
wo noch von ihren vergeblich
wirbelnden Stäben die Teller
torkeln. ....
Und plötzlich in diesem mühsamen Nirgends, plötzlich
die unsägliche Stelle, wo sich das reine Zuwenig
umbegreiflich verwandelt—, umspringt
in jenes leere Zuviel.
Wo die vielstellige Rechnung
zahlenlos aufgeht.

Plätze, o Platz in Paris, unendlicher Schauplatz,
wo die Modistin, Madame Lamort,
die ruhlosen Wege der Erde, en lose Bänder,
schlingt und windet und neue aus ihnen
Schliefen erfindet, Rüschen, Blumen, Kokarden, künstliche
Früchte—, alle unwahr gefärbt,—für die billigen
Winterhüte des Schicksals.

*

Engel!: es wäre ein Platz, den wir nicht wissen, und dorten,
auf unsäglichem Teppich, zeigten die Liebenden, die's hier
bis zum Können nie bringen, ihre kühnen
hohen Figuren des Herzschwungs,
ihre Türme aus Lust, ihre
längst, wo Boden nie war, nur aneinander
lehnenden Leitern, bebend,—und *könntens*,
vor den Zuschauern rings, unzähligen lautlosen Toten:
Würfen die dann ihre letzten, immer ersparten,
immer verborgenen, die wir nicht kennen, ewig
gültigen Münzen des Glücks vor das endlich
wahrhaft lächelnde Paar auf gestilltem Teppich?

Die Sechste Elegie

Feigenbaum, seit wie lange schon ist s mir bedeutend,
wie du die Blüte beinah ganz überschlägst
und hinein in die zeitig entschlossene Frucht,
ungerühmt, drängst dein reines Geheimnis.
Wie der Fontäne Rohr treibt dein gebognes Gezweig
abwärts den Saft und hinan: und er springt aus dem Schlaf,
fast nicht erwachend, ins Glück seiner süßesten Leistung.
Sieh: wie der Gott in den Schwan.
                         ..... Wir aber verweilen,
ach, uns rühmt es zu blühn, und ins verspätete Innre
unserer endlichen Frucht gehn wir verraten hinein.
Wenigen steigt so stark der Andrang des Handelns,
daß sie schon anstehn und glühn in der Fülle des Herzens,
wenn die Verführung zum Blühn wie gelinderte Nachtluft
ihnen die Jugend des Munds, ihnen die Lider berührt:
Helden vielleicht und den frühe Hinüberbestimmten,
denen der gärtnernde Tod anders die Adern verbiegt.
Diese stürzen dahin: dem eigenen Lächeln
sind sie voran, wie das Rossegespann in den milden
muldigen Bildern von Karnak dem siegenden König.

Wunderlich nah ist der Held doch den jugendlich Toten. Dauern
fich ihn nicht an. Sein Aufgang ist Dasein; beständig
nimmt er sich fort und tritt ins veränderte Sternbild
seiner steten Gefahr. Dort fänden ihn wenige. Aber,
das uns finster verschweigt, das plötzlich begeisterte Schicksal
singt ihn hinein in den Sturm seiner aufrauschenden Welt.

Hör ich doch keinen wie *ihn*. Auf einmal durchgeht mich
mit der strömenden Luft sein verdunkelter Ton.

Dann, wie verbärg ich mich gern vor der Sehnsucht: O wär ich,
wär ich ein Knabe und dürft es noch werden und säße
in die künftigen Arme gestützt und läse von Simson,
wie seine Mutter erst nichts und dann alles gebar.

War er nicht Held schon in dir, o Mutter, begann nicht
dort schon, in dir, seine herrische Auswahl?
Tausende brauten im Schooß und wollten *er* sein,
aber sieh: er ergriff und ließ aus, wählte und konnte.
Und wenn er Säulen zerstieß, so wars, da er ausbrach
aus der Welt deines Leibs in die engere Welt, wo er weiter

wählte und konnte. O Mütter der Helden,
o Ursprung reißender Ströme! Ihr Schluchten, in die sich
hoch von dem Herzrand, klagend,
schon die Mädchen gestürzt , künftig die Opfer dem Sohn.
Denn hinstürmte der Held durch Aufenthalte der Liebe,
jeder hob ihn hinaus, jeder ihn meinende Herzschlag,
abgewendet schon, stand er am Ende der Lächeln, anders.

Die Siebente Elegie

Werbung nicht mehr, nicht Werbung, entwachsene Stimme,
sei deines Schreies Natur; zwar schrieest due rein wie der Vogel,
wenn ihn die Jahreszeit aufhebt, die steigende,
beinah vergessend, daß er ein kümrnerndes Tier und nicht
nur ein einzelnes Herz sei, das sie ins Heitere wirft,
in die innigen Himmel. Wie er, so würbest du wohl,
nicht minder—, daß, noch unsichtbar,
dich die Freundin erführ, die stille, in der eine Antwort
langsam erwacht und über dem Hören sich anwärmt,—
deinem erkühnten Gefühl die erglühte Gefühlin.

O und der Frühling begriffe—, da ist keine Stelle,
die nicht trüge den Ton der Verkündigung. Erst jenen kleinen
fragenden Auflaut, den, mit steigernder Stille,
weithin umschweigt ein reiner bejahender Tag.
Dann die Stufen hinan, Ruf-Stufen hinan, zum geträumten
Tempel der Zukunft—; dann den Triller, Fontäne,
die zu dem drängenden Strahl schon das Fallen zuvornimmt
im versprechlichen Spiel.... Und vor sich, den Sommer.
Nicht nur die Morgen alle des Sommers—, nicht nur
wie sie sich wandeln in Tag und strahlen vor Anfang.
Nicht nur die Tage, die zart sind um Blumen, und oben,
um die gestalteten Bäume, stark und gewaltig.
Nicht nur die Andacht dieser entfalteten Kräfte,
nich nur die Wege, nicht nur die Wiesen im Abend,
nicht nur, nach spätem Gewitter, das atmende Klarsein,
nicht nur der nahende Schlaf und ein Ahnen, abends ...
sondern die Nächte! Sondern die hohen, des Sommers,
Nächte, sondern die Sterne, die Sterne der Erde.
O einst tot sein und sie wissen unendlich,
alle die Sterne: denn wie, wie, wie sie vergessen!

Siehe, da rief ich die Liebende. Aber nicht *sie* nur
Käme ... Es kämen aus schwächlichen Gräbern
Mädchen und ständen ... Denn, wie beschränk ich,
wie, den gerufenen Ruf? Die Versunkenen suchen
immer noch Erde.— Ihr Kinder, ein hiesig
einmal ergriffenes Ding gälte für viele.
Glaubt nicht, Schicksal sei mehr, als das Dichte der Kindheit;
wie überholtet ihr oft den Geliebten, atmend,
atmend nach seligem Lauf, auf nichts zu, ins Freie.

Hiersein ist herrlich. Ihr wußtet es, Mädchen, ihr auch,
die ihr scheinbar entbehrtet, versankt—, ihr, in den ärgsten
Gassen der Städte, Schwärende, oder dem Abfall
offene. Denn eine Stunde war jeder, vielleicht nicht
ganz eine Stunde, ein mit den Maßen der Zeit kaum
Meßliches swischen zwei Weilen, da sie ein Dasein
hatte. Alles. Die Adern voll Dasein.
Nur, wir vergessen so leicht, was der lachende Nachbar
uns nicht bestätigt oder beneidet. Sichtbar
wollen wirs heben, wo doch das sichtbarste Glück uns
erst zu erkennen sich gibt, wenn wir es innen verwandeln.

Nirgends, Geliebte, wird Welt sein, als innen. Unser
Leben geht hin mit Verwandlung. Und immer geringer
schwindet das Außen. Wo einmal ein dauerndes Haus war,
schlägt sich erdachtes Gebild vor, quer, zu Erdenklichem
völlig gehörig, als ständ es noch ganz im Gehirne.
Weite Speicher der Kraft, schâfft sich der Zeitgeist, gestaltlos
wie der spannende Drang, den er aus allem gewinnt.
Tempel kennt er nicht mehr. Diese, des Herzens, Verschwendung
sparen wir heimlicher ein. Ja, wo nock eins übersteht,
ein einst gebetetes Ding, ein gedientes, geknietes—,
hält es sich, so wie es ist, schon ins Unsichtbare hin.
Viele gewahrens nicht mehr, doch ohne den Vorteil,
daß sie's nun *innerlich* baun, mit Pfeilern und Statuen, größer!

Jede dumpfe Umkehr der Welt hat solche Enterbte,
denen das Frühere nicht und noch nicht das Nächste gehärt.
Denn auch das Nächste ist weit für die Menschen. Üns soll
dies nicht verwirren; es stärke in uns die Bewahrung
der noch erkannten Gestalt. Dies *stand* einmal unter Menschen,
mitten im Schicksal stands, im vernichtenden, mitten
im Nichtwissen-Wohin stand es, wie seiend, und bog
Sterne zu sich aus gesicherten Himmeln. Engel,
dir noch zeig ich es, *da*! in deinem Anschaun
steh es gerettet zuletzt, nun endlich aufrecht.
Säulen, Pylone, der Sphinx, das strebende Stemmen,
grau aus vergehender Stadt oder aus fremder, des Doms.

War es nicht Wunder? O staune, Engel, denn *wir* sinds,
wir, o du Großer, erzähls, daß wir solches vermochten, mein Atem
reicht für die Rühmung nicht aus. So haben wir dennoch
nicht die Räume versäumt, diese gewährenden, diese
unseren Räume. (Was müssen sie fürchterlich groß sein,

da sie Jahrtausende nicht unseres Fühlns überfülln.)
Aber ein Turm was groß, nicht wahr? O Engel, er war es,—
groß, auch noch neben dir? Chartres war groß—und Musik
reichte noch weiter hinan und überstieg uns. Doch selbst nur
eine Liebende—, oh, allein am nächtlichen Fenster …
reichte sie dir nicht ans Knie— ?
                              Glaub *nicht*, daß ich werbe.
Engel, und würb ich dich auch! Du kommst nicht. Denn mein
Anruf ist immer voll Hinweg; wider so starke
Strömung kannst du nicht schreiten. Wie ein gestreckter
Arm ist mein Rufen. Und seine zum Greifen
oben offene Hand bleibt vor dir
offen, wie Abwehr und Warnung,
Unfaßlicher, weitauf.

Die Achte Elegie
Rudolph Kassner zugeeignet

Mit allen Augen sieht die Kreatur
das Offene. Nur unsre Augen sind
wie umgekehrt und ganz um sie gestellt
als Fallen, rings um ihren freien Ausgang.
Was draußen *ist*, wir wissens aus des Tiers
Antlitz allein; denn schon das frühe Kind
wenden wir um und zwingens, daß es rückwärts
Gestaltung sehe, nicht das Offne, das
im Tiergesicht so tief ist. Frei von Tod.
Ihn sehen wir allein; das freie Tier
hat seinen Untergang stets hinter sich
und vor sich Gott, und wenn es geht, so gehts
in Ewigkeit, so wie die Brunnen gehen.
Wir haben nie, nicht einen einzigen Tag,
den reinen Raum vor uns, in den die Blumen
unendlich aufgehn. Immer ist es Welt
und niemals Nirgends ohne Nicht: das Reine,
Unüberwachte, das man atmet und
unendlich *weiß* und nicht begehrt. Als Kind
verliert sich eins im Stilln an dies und wird
gerüttelt. Oder jener stirbt und *ists*.
Denn nah am Tod sieht man den Tod nicht mehr
und starrt *hinaus*, vielleicht mit großem Tierblick.
Liebende, wäre nicht der andre, der
die Sicht verstellt, sind nah daran und staunen....
Wie aus Versehn is ihnen aufgetan
hinter dem andern.... Aber über ihn
kommt keiner fort, und wieder wird ihm Welt.
Der Schöpfung immer zugewendet, sehn
wir nur auf ihr die Spiegelung des Frein,
von uns verdunkelt. Oder das ein Tier,
ein stummes, aufschaut, ruhig durch uns durch.
Dieses heißt Schicksal: gegenüber sein
und nichts als das und immer gegenüber.

Wäre Bewußtheit unsrer Art in dem
sicheren Tier, das uns entgegenzieht
in anderer Richtung—, riß es uns herum
mit seinem Wandel. Doch sein Sein ist ihm
unendlich, ungefaßt und ohne Blick
auf seinen Zustand, rein, so wie sein Ausblick.

Und wo wir Zukunft sehn, dort sieht es Alles
und sich in Allem und geheilt für immer.
Und doch ist in dem wachsam warmen Tier
Gewicht und Sorge einer großen Schwermut
Denn ihm auch haftet immer an, was uns
oft überwältigt, —die Erinnerung,
als sei schon einmal das, wonach man drängt,
näher gewesen, treuer und sein Anschluß
unendlich zärtlich. Hier ist alles Abstand,
und dort wars Atem. Nach der ersten Heimat
ist ihm die zweite zwitterig und windig.
O Seligkeit der *kleinen* Kreatur,
die immer *bleibt* im Schooße, der sie austrug;
o Glück der Mücke, die noch *innen* hüpft,
selbst wenn sie Hochzeit hat: denn Schooß ist Alles.
Und sieh die halbe Sicherheit des Vogels,
der beinah beides weiß aus seinem Ursprung,
als wär er eine Seele der Etrusker,
aus einem Toten, den ein Raum empfing,
doch mit der ruhenden Figur als Deckel.
Und wie bestürzt ist eins, das fliegen muß
und stammt aus einem Schooß. Wie vor sich selbst
erschreckt, durchzuckts die Luft, wie wenn ein Sprung
durch eine Tasse geht. So reißt die Spur
der Fledermaus durchs Porzellan des Abends.

Und wir: Zuschauer, immer, überall,
dem allen zugewandt und nie hinaus!
Uns überfüllts. Wir ordnens. Es zerfällt.
Wir ordnens wieder und zerfallen selbst.

Wer hat uns also umgedreht, daß wir,
was wir auch tun, in jener Haltung sind
von einem, welcher fortgeht? Wie er auf
dem letzten Hügel, der ihm ganz sein Tal
noch einmal zeigt, sich wendet, anhält, weilt—,
so leben wir und nehmen immer Abschied.

Die Neunte Elegie

Warum, wenn es angeht, also die Frist des Daseins
hinzubringen, als Lorbeer, ein wenig dunkler als alle
andere Grün, mit kleinen Wellen an jedem
Blattrand (wie eines Windes Lächeln)—: warum dann
Menschliches müssen—und, Schicksal vermeidend,
sich sehnen nach Schicksal?...
                           Oh, *nicht*, weil Glück *ist*,
dieser voreilige Vorteil eines nahen Verlusts.
Nicht aus Neugier, oder zur Übung des Herzens,
das auch im Lorbeer *wäre* .....

Aber weil Hiersein viel ist, und weil uns scheinbar
alles das Hiesige braucht, dieses Schwindende, das
seltsam uns angeht. Uns, die Schwindendsten. *Ein*mal
jedes, nur *cin* Mal. *Ein*mal und nichtmehr. Und wir auch
einmal. Nie wieder. Aber dieses
einmal gewesen zu sein, wenn auch nur *ein*mal:
irdisch gewesen zu sein, scheint nicht widerrufbar.

Und so drängen wir uns und wollen es leisten,
wollens enthalten in unsern einfachen Händen,
im überfüllteren Blick und im sprachlosen Herzen.
Wollen es werden. Wem es geben? Am liebsten
alles behalten fur immer ... Ach, in den andern Bezug,
wehe, was nimmt man hinüber? Nicht das Anschaun, das hier
langsam erlernte, und kein hier Ereignetes. Keins.
Also die Schmerzen. Also vor allem das Schwersein,
also der Liebe lange Erfahrung,—also
lauter Unsägliches. Aber später,
unter den Sternen, was solls: *die* sind *besser* unsäglich.
Bringt doch der Wanderer auch vom Hange des Bergrands
nicht eine Hand voll Erde ins Tal, die Allen unsagliche, sondern
ein erworbenes Wort, reines, den gelben und blaun
Enzian. Sind wir vielleicht *hier*, um zu sagen: Haus,
Brucke, Brunnen, Tor, Krug, Obstbaum, Fenster,—
hochstens: Säule, Turm ... aber zu *sagen*, verstehs,
oh zu sagen *so*, wie selber die Dinge niemals
innig meinten zu sein. Ist nicht die heimliche List
dieser verschwiegenen Erde, wenn sie die Liebenden drängt,
daß sich in ihrem Gefühl jedes und jedes entzückt?
Schwelle: was ists für zwei
Liebende, daß sie die eigne ältere Schwelle der Tür

ein wenig verbrauchen, auch sie, nach den vielen vorher
und vor den Künftigen ..., leicht.

Hier ist des *Säglichen* Zeit, *hier* seine Heimat.
Sprich und bekenn. Mehr als je
fallen die Dinge dahin, die erlebbaren, denn,
was sie verdrängend ersetzt, ist ein Tun ohne Bild.
Tun unter Krusten, die willig zerspringen, sobald
innen das Handeln entwächst und sich anders begrenzt.
Zwischen den Hämmern besteht
unser Herz, wie die Zunge
zwischen den Zähnen, die doch,
dennoch, die preisende bleibt.

Preise dem Engel die Welt, nicht die unsägliche, *ihm*
kannst du nicht großtun mit herrlich Erfühltem; im Weltall,
wo er fühlender fühlt, bist du ein Neuling. Drum zeig
ihm das Einfache, das, von Geschlecht zu Geschlechtern
gestaltet, als ein Unsriges lebt, neben der Hand und im Blick.
Sag ihm die Dinge. Er wird staunender stehn; wie du standest
bei dem Seiler in Rom, oder bein Töpfer am Nil. Zeig ihm,
wie glücklich ein Ding wein kann, wie schuldlos und unser,
wie selbst das klagende Leid rein zur Gestalt sich entschließt,
dient als ein Ding, oder stirbt in ein Ding—, und jenseits
selig der Geige entgeht. Und diese, von Hingang
lebenden Dinge verstehn, daß du sie rühmst; vergänglich,
traun sie ein Rettendes uns, den Vergänglichsten, zu.
Wollen, wir sollen sie ganz im unsichtbarn Herzen verwandeln
in—o unendlich—in uns! Wer wir am Ende auch seien.

Erde, ist es nicht dies, was du willst: *unsichtbar*
in uns erstehn?— Ist es dein Traum nicht,
einmal unsichtbar zu sein? —Erde! unsichtbar!
Was, wenn Verwandlung nicht, ist dein drängender Auftrag?
Erde, du liebe, ich will. Oh glaub, es bedürfte
nicht deiner Frühlinge mehr, mich dir zu gewinnen, einer
ach, ein einziger ist schon dem Blute zu viel.
Namenlos bin ich zu dir entschlossen, von weit her.
Immer warst du im Recht, und dein heiliger Einfall
ist der vertrauliche Tod.
Siehe, ich lebe. Woraus? Weder Kindheit noch Zukunft
werden weniger ..... Überzähliges Dasein
entspringt mir im Herzen.

Die Zehnte Elegie

Daß ich dereinst, an dem Ausgang der grimmigen Einsicht,
Jubel und Ruhm aufsinge zustimmenden Engeln.
Daß von den klar geschlagenen Hämmern des Herzens
keiner versage an weichen, zweifelnden oder
reißenden Saiten. Daß mich mein strömendes Antlitz
glänzender mache; daß das unscheinbare Weinen
blühe. O wie werdet ihr dann, Nächte, mir lieb sein,
gehärmte. Daß ich euch knieender nicht, untröstliche Schwestern,
hinnahm, nicht in euer gelöstes
Haar mich gelöster ergab. Wir, Vergeuder der Schmerzen.
Wie wir sie absehn voraus, in die traurige Dauer,
ob sie nicht enden vielleicht. Sie aber sind ja
unser winterwähriges Laub, unser dunkeles Sinngrün,
eine der Zeiten des heimlichen Jahres—, nicht nur
Zeit—, sind Stelle, Siedelung, Lager, Boden, Wohnort.

Freilich, wehe, wie fremd sind die Gassen der Leid-Stadt,
wo in der falschen, aus Übertönung gemachten
Stille, stark, aus der Gußform des Leeren der Ausguß
prahlt der vergoldete Lärm, das platzende Denkmal.
O, wie spurlos zerträte ein Engel ihnen den Trostmarkt,
den die Kirche begrenzt, ihre fertig gekaufte:
reinlich und zu und enttäuscht wie ein Postamt am Sonntag.
Draußen aber kräuseln sich immer die Ränder von Jahrmarkt.
Schaukeln der Freiheit! Taucher und Gaukler des Eifers!
Und des behübschten Glücks figürliche Schießstatt,
wo es zappelt von Ziel und sich blechern benimmt,
wenn ein Geschickterer trifft. Von Beifall zu Zufall
taumelt er weiter; denn Buden jeglicher Neugier werben,
trommeln und plärrn. Für Erwachsene aber ist noch
besonders zu sehn, wie das Geld sich vermehrt, anatomisch,
nicht zur Belustigung nur: der Geschlechtsteil des Gelds,
alles, das Ganze, der Vorgang—, das unterrichtet und macht
fruchtbar ....
                    ... Oh aber gleich darüber hinaus,
hinter der letzten Planke, bekelbt mit Plakaten des "Todlos,"
jenes bitteren Biers, das den Trinkenden süß scheint,
wenn sie immer dazu frische Zerstreuungen kaun ...,
gleich im Rücken der Planke, gleich dahinter, ists *wirklich*.
Kinder spielen, und Liebende halten einander, —abseits,
ernst, im ärmlichen Gras, und Hunde haben Natur.
Weiter noch zieht es den Jüngling; vielleicht, daß er eine junge

Klage liebt … Hinter ihr her kommt er in Wiesen. Sie sagt:
Weit. Wir wohnen dort draußen….
                                        Wo? Und der Jüngling
folgt. Ihn rührt ihre Haltung. Die Schulter, der Hals—, vielleicht
ist sie von herrlicher Herkunft. Aber er läßt sie, kehrt um,
wendet sich, winkt … Was solls? Sie ist eine Klage.

Nur die jungen Toten, im ersten Zustand
zeitlosen Gleichmuts, dem der Entwöhnung,
folgen ihr liebend. Mädchen
wartet sie ab und befreundet sie. Zeigt ihnen leise,
was sie an sich hat. Perlen des Leids und die feinen
Schleier der Duldung. —Mit Jünglingen geht sie schweigend.

Aber dort, wo sie wohnen, im Tal, der Älteren eine, der Klagen,
nimmt sich des Jünglinges an, wenn er fragt: —Wirwaren,
sagt wie, ein großes Geschlecht, einmal, wir Klagen. Die Väter
trieben den Bergbau dort in dem großen Gebirg; bei Menschen
findest du manchmal ein Stück geschliffenes Urleid
oder, aus altem Vulkan, schlackig versteinerten Zorn.
Ja, das stammte von dort. Einst waren wir reich.—

Und sie leitet ihn leicht durch die weite Landschaft der Klagen,
zeigt ihm die Säulen der Tempel oder die Triimmer
jener Burgen, von wo Klage-Fürsten das Land
einstens weise beherrscht. Zeigt ihm die hohen
Tränenbäume und Felder blühender Wehmut,
(Lebendige kennen sie nur als sanftes Blattwerk); zeigt ihm
die Tiere der Trauer, weidend, —und manchmal schreckt
ein Vogel und zieht, flach ihnen fliegend durchs Aufschaun
weithin das schriftliche Bild seines vereinsamten Schreis.—
Abends führt sie ihn hin zu den Gräbern der Alten
aus dem Klage-Geschlecht, den Sibyllen und Warn-Herrn.
Naht aber Nacht, so wandeln sie leiser, und bald
mondets empor, das über alles
wachende Grab-Mal. Brüderlich jenem am Nil,
der erhabene Sphinx—: der verschwiegenen Kammer Antlitz.
Und sie staunen dem krönlichen Haupt, das für immer,
schweigend, der Menschen Gesicht
auf die Waage der Sterne gelegt.

Nicht erfaßt es sein Blick, irn Frühtod
schwindelnd. Aber ihr Schaun,
hinter dem Pschent-Rand hervor, scheucht es die Eule. Und sie,

streifend im langsamen Abstrich die Wange entlang,
jene der reifes ten Rundung,
zeichnet weich in das neue

Totengehör, über ein doppelt
aufgeschlagenes Blatt, den unbeschreiblichen Umriß.

Und höher, die Sterne. Neue. Die Sterne des Leidlands.
Langsam nennt sie die Klage: « Hier,
siehe: den *Reiter*, den *Stab*, und das vollere Sternbild
nennen sie: *Fruchthranz*. Dann, weiter, dem Pol zu:
Wiege; Weg; Das Brennende Buch; Puppe; Fenster.
Aber im südlichen Himmel, rein wie im Innern
einer gesegneten Hand, das klar erglänzende *M*,
das die Mütter bedeutet..... »

Doch der Tot muß fort, und schweigend bringt ihn die ältere
Klage bis an die Talschlucht,
wo es schimmert im Mondschein:
die Quelle der Freude. In Ehrfurcht
nennt sie sie, sagt: « Bei den Menschen
ist sie ein tragender Strom. »

Stehn am Fuß des Gebirgs.
Und da umarmt sie ihn, weinend.
Einsam steigt er dahin, in die Berge des Urleids.
Und nicht einmal sein Schritt klingt aus dem tonlosen Los.

*

Aber erweckten sie uns, die unendlich Toten, ein Gleichnis,
siehe, sie zeigten vielleicht auf die Kätzchen der leeren
Hasel, die hängenden, oder
meinten den Regen, der fällt auf dunkles Erdreich im Frühjahr. —

Und wir, die an *steigendes* Glück denken,
empfänden die Rührung,
die uns beinah bestürzt,
wenn ein Glückliches *fällt*.

Sheryl Massaro is an oil painter, poet, and photographer based in Frederick, MD. She holds an MFA in Creative Writing/Poetry from The American University and studied with several key poets, including Allen Ginsberg, Stanley Kunitz, W.S. Merwin, et al. Her other books include two collections of her poetry: *afloat–a raft of water poems* and *a generation –30 years of poetry*.

Massaro's visual art and poetry, though often based on the recognizable, share a deeper, "off to the side" look at life than the purely representational. In each of these arts, she taps into and conveys life's undertow—the unspoken, unseen energy that binds artists and their readers or viewers.

For information on Massaro's books and art, please visit sherylmassaro.com.